LEFT FIELD, RELOADED

More Cartoons
by
Randy Halford

authorHOUSE®

AuthorHouse™
1663 Liberty Drive
Bloomington, IN 47403
www.authorhouse.com
Phone: 1-800-839-8640

First published by AuthorHouse 02/23/2010

ISBN:978-1-4490-7503-3 (sc)
ISBN:978-1-4490-7504-0 (e)

Library Congress Number:2010901345

Printed in the United States of America
Bloomington, Indiana

This book is printed on acid-free paper.

THANKS...

To AuthorHouse for helping me through my sophomore book.

To those who have read my first book, and urged me to do a second one (as if I could ever refuse!).

"If 'Seinfeld' is a television show about nothing, then 'Left Field' are cartoons about everything else."
 —Randy Halford

More Cartoons by RANDY HALFORD

1

THE POTATOHEADS AT HOME

2

3

4

THE HORSES OF "BONANZA"

"..DANGIT, JASON! WE CAN NEVER TELL
WHEN YOU'RE BLUFFIN'..."

"CAREFUL THERE, SON—DON'T WOOF DOWN YOUR FOOD."

7

GODZILLA: THE EARLY YEARS

8

"..HELLO? KELSEY'S MARKET? DO YOU
HAVE SARDINES IN A CAN? WELL, PLEASE
LET 'EM OUT--THEY'RE COUSINS OF MINE..."

HORSE MEETINGS

10

THE WONDER BREAD FAMILY

11

SCHOOL FOR THE MIS-DIRECTED

12

THE LESS-SUSPENSEFUL SEQUEL TO "ARACHNA-
PHOBIA"—"GERBILPHOBIA"...

13

14

TIRED OF BEING A "SLY" FOX, AXEL DECIDES TO TAKE THE DIRECT APPROACH...

15

16

"DRACULA: THE MUSICAL"

17

18

19

20

CATERPILLAR FUNERALS

21

23

"OH, STOP WORRYING, HERB, AND COME ENJOY THE SUN! IT'S NOT AS IF YOU WON'T PEEL EVENTUALLY!"

24

THE INNER-CITY PUNKS SOON REGRETTED THEIR
DECISION TO DEFACE THE FAMOUS "HEE-HAW" FENCE...

25

FLEA INSULTS

26

LUKE SKYWALKER'S CHILDHOOD

27

WHEN THE WICKED WITCH CLEANS HOUSE

28

29

30

ARTIST: RANDY HALFORD
TITLE: I WAS IN A REALLY WEIRD MOOD; SO SUE ME.

31

PRIMITIVE HAIRPIECES

32

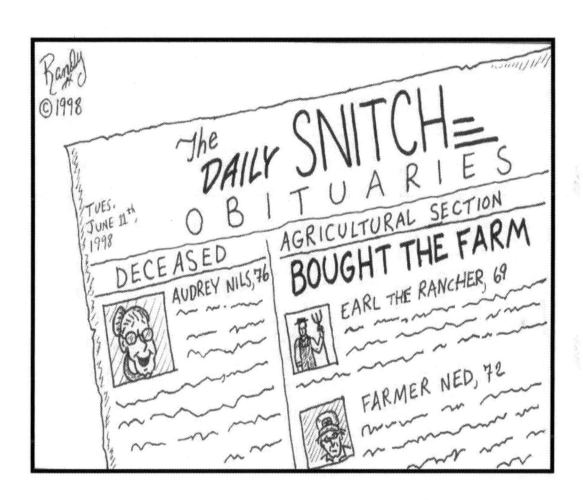

33

34

FROM THE OLD IRON CURTAIN DAYS: THE RUSSIAN BLUES

35

"I CAN NEVER LIE TO MY WIFE. I ALWAYS COME HOME WITH THAT 'HUMAN-CAUGHT-IN-THE-HEADLIGHTS' LOOK".

36

ECONOMY FLIGHTS

37

ON THE WAY TO THE NERD CONVENTION

38

HUMPTY'S EPITAPH

39

40

BESSIE'S NIGHT OUT

41

42

TWISTER TANTRUMS

43

"AND NOW, FOLKS, IT'S TIME TO PRESENT OUR GUEST OF HONOR. SO WON'T YOU PUT YOUR LEGS TOGETHER FOR A SUPER GUY...!"

44

MOSES' HECKLERS

45

"STAR WARS:
THE PHANTOM DENNIS-THE-MENACE"

46

47

AMOEBA MARRIAGE COUNSELLING

48

49

"SO! WHICH ONE O' YA SIDEWINDERS IS BILLY THE KID?!"

50

MR. ED: THE TWILIGHT YEARS

51

SANTA KNEW THE ELVES HAD GONE OUT FOR A JOY-
RIDE THE NIGHT BEFORE WHEN HE DISCOVERED A
MINI-BRA IN THE SLEIGH...

52

WHEN GOD CREATED HYENAS

53

54

"WELL, MR. BUZZOFF, SEEMS LIKE YOU'VE CAUGHT A DANDY CASE OF THE HIVES..."

55

COD-NEY DANGERFIELD

57

ACTOR LEONARDO DECAPITATED

58

GARDENING HORROR FILMS

59

T.V.'S "MAD ABOUT EWE"

60

61

62

THE BEACH BUOYS

63

64

FLY MOVIES

65

CLOWN FISH

66

"CELL" PHONES

67

THE LED ZEPPELIN MALL

68

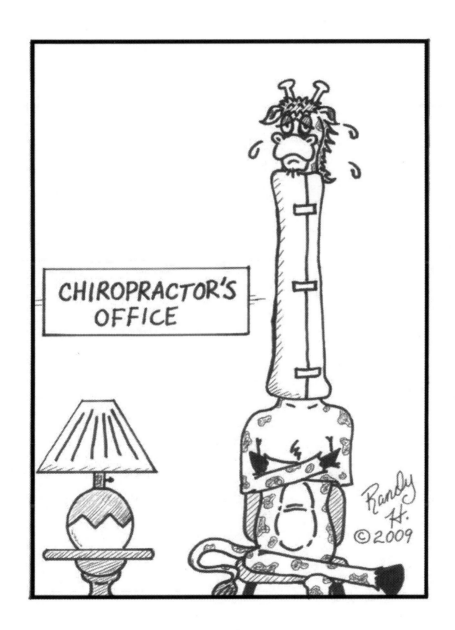

69

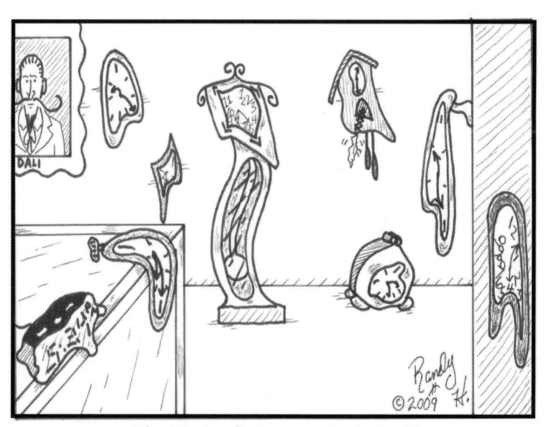

THE SALVADOR DALI CLOCK SHOP

70

MILLI VANILLI'S DOG

71

72

WILLIAM SHAKESPEARE TITLING HIS PLAYS

74

75

CORAL BURNETT

76

... AND SO, I CONTINUED TO FLOAT DOWN THE LONG, DARK, EMPTY HALLWAY...
WHEN SUDDENLY...
THERE APPEARED THE DISGUSTING APPARITION OF A WARM-BLOODED HUMAN! I FROZE IN MY TRACKS, AND AN ICY COLD SHIVER RAN UP AND DOWN MY SHEET...!

CLICK
CLICK
TAP

Randy
H.
©2009

GHOST WRITERS

77

CRAB MUSICALS

78

79

PABLO PICASSO'S FAMILY PORTRAIT

80

81

82

83

AS FLIGHT 913 SLOWLY SANK TO A WATERY GRAVE, ITS SURVIVORS WERE FORTUNATE THAT CELEBRITY PASSENGER JULIA ROBERTS' LIPS COULD BE USED AS A FLOATATION DEVICE...

84

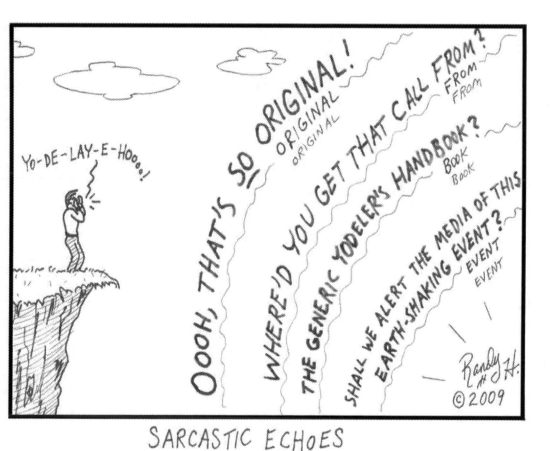

SARCASTIC ECHOES

85

COUNT CHOCULA'S MIDNIGHT CRAVINGS

86

ZOOOOOOm!

"THE FLYING NUN'S" BETTER AND FASTER COUSIN, "THE FLYING STEALTH NUN"

87

THE
BROOM HILDA
INSOMNIA
CENTER
FOR
WITCHES
DEDICATED TO CURING
"NO REST
FOR THE WICKED"

Randy H.
©2009

88

JAVA DRAMAS

89

IN THIS SCENE FROM "THE MATRIX: RECREATIONS", NEO AND HIS DOG ENJOY SOME FRISBEE IN THE PARK...

90

91

ZOMBIE LOVE

92

KING KONG DROPS HIS CELL PHONE

93

SURROUNDED BY SHINY PERFECT COMPANIONS ON
THE WALL, CUTTER THE GARDENING SHEARS SOON
REALIZED HE WASN'T "THE SHARPEST TOOL IN THE SHED"...

94

A PARROT'S TRAIN OF THOUGHT

95

THE BIG BAD WOLF PREPARES FOR THE THREE LITTLE PIGS

96

THE T.V. CRIME DRAMA "CSI: CAIRO"

98

"THE OLD WOMAN WHO LIVES IN A SHOE" GETS A HOME MAKEOVER

99

COMMON SPORTS AFFLICTIONS

100

RHINO-PLASTY

101

THE JUDGES BEGAN TO SUSPECT THAT SOMEONE CREATED AN
UNFAIR ADVANTAGE BY BRINGING IN A "WEAPON OF INTIMIDATION";
ELIJAH WOOD AND HIS DINNER PLATE-SIZED EYES...

102

JUST ASKING FOR TROUBLE

103

104

T.V.'S "DANCING WITH THE STARFISH"

105

106

POULTRY MOVIES

107

RETIREMENT HOME PRANKS

108

BEAVER PRODIGIES

109

COWARD SCHOOL

110

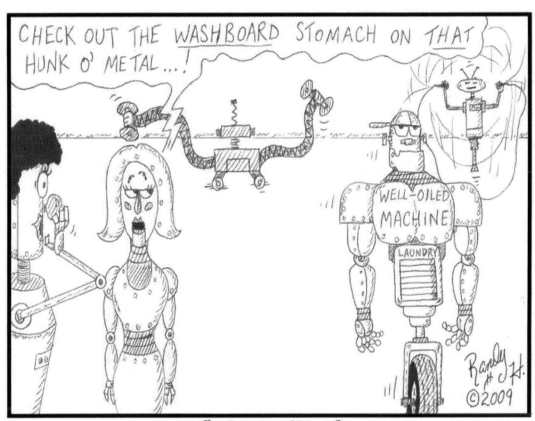

ROBOT GYMS

111

A COMMON PROBLEM AMONG MAGICIANS: IN-GROWN HARES...

112

"IT'S NO USE, DOC! I'VE TRIED EVERYTHING--FIXING THE SPHINX'S NOSE--SCARING TOURISTS--BUT I JUST CAN'T SEEM TO UNWIND..."

THE EVOLUTIONARY CHART OF LAWYERS

114

115

NO COMMENT

116

SCENE FROM "HARRY POTTER AND THE VENGEFUL BROOM"

117

BILL MURRAY: TALK SHOW HOST

118

MANKIND'S EARLY CAVE DRAWINGS OF FOOD

119

GARFIELD THE CAT'S INTERVENTION

120

CLOSE ENCOUNTERS OF THE DELICATE KIND

121

HOW HUMMINGBIRDS PREPARE FOR THE DAY

122

CLOWN FUNERALS

124

CLOWN FUNERALS, PART 2

125

WAGON TRAIN BUMPER STICKERS

126

TOM THUMB'S SHOWBIZ UNCLE

127

WHY COCKROACH SURPRISE PARTIES NEVER WORK

128

DAVID LETTERMAN'S CHILDHOOD

129

130

131

132

COW FLICKS

133

134

BULL SESSIONS

135

FRUIT MOOD MUSIC

136

137

138

THE FOLLOW-UP TO THE HORROR FILM "THE HILLS HAVE EYES":
THE STRAIGHT-TO-VIDEO "THE ROADS HAVE NOSES"

139

140

DENTAL GAME SHOWS

141

HOW SMALL DOGS GET THEIR HIGH-PITCHED BARKS

142

143

144

145

146

"...LADIES AND GENTLEMEN, WE JUST RECEIVED WORD THERE'S A MUSIC LEGEND IN OUR AUDIENCE TONIGHT. LET'S SEE IF WE CAN FIND MISS DIANA ROSS...!"

147

SID'S FATE WAS SEALED: THE MOB SENT THEIR BEST
HITMAN--EDDIE "THE ERASER" LINGUINI--TO "RUB HIM OUT"...

148

149

BLOODY DEATH OF A SALESMAN

THE ICE PICK COMETH

© 2009 Randy H.

OKLAHOMA MASSACRE!

SEVEN BEATINGS FOR SEVEN BROTHERS

P.S. —YOUR CAT IS SHOT, STABBED, SKINNED, AND FINALLY, DEAD

VIOLENT BROADWAY

150

151

ROBBIN' WILLIAMS

152

MOSQUITO LEISURE TIME

153

THE R-RATED VERSION OF "WHERE THE WILD THINGS ARE"

154

155

"DANCE UNTIL THE COWS COME HOME" THROUGH THE
DECADES

156

A LEGENDARY NEWSMAN'S EPITAPH

MERRY X-MAS!

©2009

158

159

THE BEATLES' "ABBEY ROAD" COVER: THE YOKO ONO EDITION

160

THE DR. SEUSS CLASSIC "HORTON HEARS THE WHO"

161

THE OPERATION WAS GOING SPLENDID UNTIL THE UNTHINK-
ABLE HAPPENED: THE CHIEF SURGEON WAS SUDDENLY STRICKEN
WITH "JAZZ HANDS"...

162

CAT HELL

163

DOG HEAVEN

164

165